Acknowledgments

The authors would like to extend their warmest thanks
to the children who agreed to act as models for this book:
Albéric Chambert, Victoire Chambert,
Balsamie Deleval, Flavie Deleval,
Quitterie Genevray, and Victoire Le Touzé.

Translator's note

All the craft supplies mentioned in this book are available in art
and craft supply stores in the United States. Abaca is available in
millinery suppliers. In adapting the recipes, American ingredients
were substituted for French ones whenever possible. Every effort
was made to convert the measurements for the craft projects and
the recipes to standard American measures.

First edition for the United States and Canada published by
Barron's Educational Series, Inc., 2000.

All inquiries should be addressed to:
Barron's Educational Series, Inc.
250 Wireless Boulevard
Hauppauge, New York 11788
http: //www.barronseduc.com

Library of Congress Catalog Card No. 00-102971

International Standard Book No. 0-7641-1625-8

Printed in Hong Kong

9 8 7 6 5 4 3 2 1

Graphic Designers: Claire Brenier and Hervé Tardy
Layout: Lélie Carnot
Editor: Frédérique Crestin-Billet
Editorial Assistant: Martine Roccard
Illustrations: Jean-Luc Guérin
Story by Pierre Juziers
Makeup by Marie Chantal
Recipes by Charlotte Genevray and Beverly Bennett

HALLOWEEN
imaginative holiday ideas

Marie-Laure Mantoux
Frédérique Crestin-Billet

Photographs
Fanny Bruno

Translated and Adapted by
Myriam Chapman

BARRON'S

The Story of Halloween

Everybody knows what Halloween is: ghosts, goblins, witches on broomsticks, grinning jack-o'-lanterns, scary costumes, trick or treat, or having a great party at home with your friends on the night of October 31.

But did you know that Halloween is really an ancient celebration that may have started as far back as three thousand years ago among a tribe of people called the Celts? The Celts lived in England, Ireland, Scotland, Wales, and parts of France. According to the Celtic calendar, October 31 was the exact day summer ended and the new year began. The harvest was in and animals were back in their stables. The Celts believed that on this night, people who had died during the year came back to earth for a short visit among the living. It was a scary time and the Celtic priests, called Druids, participated in a special ceremony to ensure good luck during the coming year. They put out the sacred fire that had burned all year on the altar and started a new one, using the branches of the sacred oak tree. This fire, dedicated to the god of the sun, was meant to scare away the evil spirits. The Druids carried a lighted branch from house to house and used it to kindle a new fire in each household. In this way, the village was safe for another year. During this ritual, called the feast of Samhain, the villagers wore hideous costumes and made terrible faces to scare away the evil spirits.

The celebration of Samhain lasted eight days. Much later, during the Middle Ages, the Roman Catholic Church frowned on such pagan celebrations. November 1 was designated a religious holiday known as All Saints' Day. In England, All Saints' Day was known as All Hallows, and the night before was known as All Hallows' Eve. In certain parts of Ireland, England, Scotland, and Wales, the old customs associated with the Celtic rituals were still kept, and the night of October 31 became known as Halloween.

During the nineteenth century, people from Ireland and the British Isles immigrated to this country, bringing with them the traditions and symbols of Halloween. One of the most popular was the jack-o'-lantern. This grinning pumpkin may have its origins in a legend about a man named Jack who was foolish enough to play practical jokes on the Devil. Chased out of paradise because he enjoyed the Devil's company, and kicked out of the lower depths because he played jokes on the Devil, Jack was condemned to wander the earth until Judgment Day, carrying a lighted twig he had placed inside a carved-out turnip.

Over time and in the telling, Jack and his turnip became a jack-o'-lantern. That's how legends grow, borrowing from here and there.

Halloween became a recognized holiday in the United States towards the end of the nineteenth century. But in the early 1800s, Halloween wasn't only a time of fun. People engaged in pranks that were not so pleasant. The tradition of trick or treat didn't start until the 1930s. So today, instead of lighting a fire to ward off the evil spirits, people give candies and other treats to children in fantastic costumes who come knocking at their door. That's how an ancient custom turned into the special fun time that is today's Halloween.

CONTENTS

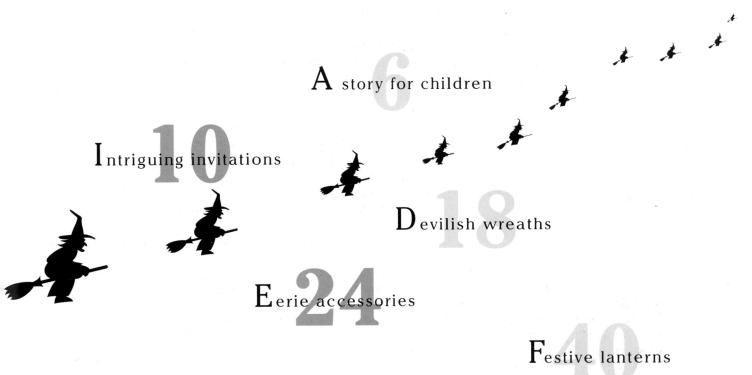

The Halloween Star

A hundred years ago, in the little Norwegian town of Molden, children were celebrating Halloween in their own way. It was a cold and dry November evening, but their shouts and laughter echoed through the streets, which were lined with red and green snow-covered wooden houses.

Knock knock! A small child wearing a scary mask knocked at the door of one of those brightly colored houses and called out, "It's Halloween!" A friendly woman answered the door and handed the child a package of candies or a krone, which is Norwegian money.

All around the town, you could hear boys and girls happily shouting, "It's Halloween!" as they went from door to door.

Christen and Clara had gathered enough goodies for this Halloween evening. They paused to look up at the star-studded sky.

"The sky is so beautiful tonight. It's covered with stars," said Clara. "It makes me sad to think the stars are so far away."

Christen looked up at the sky, too.

"You're right," he said. "It is too bad. You know what I would like? I'd like to catch a star!"

"Are you crazy?" said Clara. "That's impossible!"

"See the North Star up there? That's my favorite. What if we begged the North Star to come down to us for a visit?"

Clara burst out laughing.

"Well, we could always try," she said.

Then brother and sister recited together, just for fun:

> We beseech you, Northern Star
> Pay us a visit from afar.
> You shine so brightly in the sky
> Come down from your perch up high.

And they waited.

Suddenly, from the depth of the starry sky, they saw a point of bright light get brighter and brighter as it came closer and closer to earth. It was the North Star answering their call. In just a few minutes, the star fell quietly at their feet.

At first, Christen and Clara were very frightened.

"Be careful—it could burn you!"

"I thought it would be bigger!"

They ran home as fast as they could to get a big box and some cotton with which to line it. Luckily, the star was still there when they returned.

Very, very carefully, they placed the star in the box and carried the box back home. They were so proud of their treasure!

The star lay without burning in the box. It was clear that it was a friendly star and not a dangerous one. But how were Christen and Clara to explain this extraordinary event to their parents?

Just before getting into bed, Christen said to his parents, very casually, "Look up at the sky, Mama and Papa! Don't you notice something strange up there?"

Indeed, the night was very beautiful, his parents said, but that was probably because it was Halloween. Other than that, neither his mother nor his father saw anything different in the night sky.

"Well," said Clara, who could sometimes be a little snippy. "You must not be looking very carefully."

"We are," said her father. "What is there to see?"

"Well, look closely at the sky. The North Star is missing!"

"You're right," said her mother. "Isn't that strange. I don't see the North Star."

Christen could not help shouting gleefully, "It's not at all strange. You can't find the star in the sky because it's not there. It's down here."

"What do you mean, down here?" said his father.

"Down here, with us, in our house," Clara answered.

Then Christen ran into his room, took the box with the star inside, and showed it to his parents.

"Look. Isn't this the North Star? Now what do you have to say?"

"Amazing," said the children's parents. "How did you manage to capture it?"

"We didn't capture it. We just thought this star was so beautiful that we begged it to come down to earth for a visit, and that's what it did."

At school the following day, the teacher asked the children to tell about their most wonderful memory of Halloween. Christen raised his hand and the teacher called on him.

Christen told his story, but his classmates and his teacher didn't quite believe him.

"You think I'm making this up," said Christen. "Tomorrow I'll bring you the North Star, and then you'll see that I'm telling the truth."

And that is what he did.

Christen brought the star to school the next day. As soon as he opened the box, his friends were amazed. They couldn't stop asking questions.

"Is it sharp?"

"Does it burn?"

"Does it shine as brightly down here as it does in the sky?"

"Do you think it can survive on earth? Will it burn out and die?"

Thus it was that for the next few weeks, children, teachers, and friends young and old gathered in front of the city hall to admire the miraculous star, which had been hung there for all to see. Because it was a miracle, wasn't it? That sort of thing just didn't happen every day.

Soon the newspapers (television didn't exist in those days) were full of accounts of the strange occurrence. Little by little, the whole world learned that on the night of Halloween, two children had made a star come down to earth.

Three weeks later, Clara, who was very observant, called her brother's attention to something disturbing.

"Look at our star," she said. "Don't you think it's different somehow?"

"No, I don't think so."

"Well, I think it is not as bright as before. Look closely."

"Yes, you're right. It's shining less brightly than on the first day. Maybe visiting earth isn't so good for a star. Do you think it's going to die?"

"Oh, no. That would be too sad."

That night, the children didn't get much sleep. They thought and thought about their star. In the morning, Clara said to Christen, "I've been thinking all night. This star doesn't seem very happy. Maybe it misses its home in the sky. A fish would miss his home if we took him out of the water, so why not a star?"

"Well, what should we do?"

"I have an idea. Tonight, let's place our star on the windowsill. Let's leave the top off the box so that it can breathe more easily and so that it can see the sky."

Christen agreed that this was a good plan. Before going to bed the following night, the children placed the open box on the windowsill.

"I hope it doesn't catch cold."

"Of course not. It's used to the cold. Up there, it's much colder than down here." And so they fell asleep.

The following morning, when they woke up, the box was empty. Tired of being alone on earth, far from its brother and sister stars, the star had gone back to its place in the sky.

In the evening, the children said to their parents, "Look at the sky tonight. There's been another miracle."

The father and the mother looked up at the night sky.

"The North Star! It's back."

"That's right. It didn't seem very happy, so we decided to give it its freedom."

This second event again created a stir all over Norway. No one could recall ever seeing a star that came down to earth, allowed itself to be put on display, and then returned to the night sky. That's why, from that day on, the people of Molden called the North Star the Halloween Star, in honor of its extraordinary journey to earth.

INTRIGUING
I N V I T A T I O N S

Let witches and spiders, pumpkins and bats invite your friends to the party. These invitations reflect the spirit of Halloween.

Twelve-witch invitation

- **Pencil**
- **Orange card stock, 16 × 8 inches (40 cm × 20 cm)**
- **Black card stock, 6 × 8 inches (15 cm × 20 cm)**
- **White glue**
- **Witch silhouette rubber stamp**
- **Three-witch rubber stamp**
- **Black ink stamp pad**
- **Black marker**
- **Pinking shears or paper edgers**

1 Draw an irregular oval, 7 × 5½ inches (18 cm × 14 cm), on the orange card stock. Draw a slightly smaller oval, 5½ × 4 inches (14 cm × 10 cm), on the same piece of card stock. On the black card stock, draw another irregular oval, 6 × 4½ inches (16 cm × 12 cm).

Cut the ovals out with pinking shears or paper edgers to scallop the edges. Glue the black oval over the biggest orange oval and the smaller orange oval over the black one.

2 Ink the witch stamp and stamp nine witches around the circumference of the top orange oval. Stamp the three witches in the center. Fill in the witch figures with a black marker. Your twelve witches will set the creepy tone of your party!

Ghost invitation

- **White craft foam, 8 × 8 inches (20 cm × 20 cm)**
- **Bristol board, 8 × 8 inches (20 cm × 20 cm)**
- **Tracing paper**
- **Two small plastic eyes**
- **Nontoxic glue**
- **Craft knife or scissors**

Glue the craft foam to the bristol board, using nontoxic glue.

Trace the ghost pattern on page 16 and transfer it carefully to the bristol board. Cut the ghost shape out, using the craft knife or a pair of scissors.

Glue the plastic eyes to the ghost on the craft foam side. Use the bristol board side to write out the invitation.

If you can't find plastic eyes, cut two circles out of black card stock or poster board. Your ghost will look just as spooky.

Spiderweb invitation

- **Textured white drawing paper,
  8 × 8 inches (20 cm × 20 cm)**
- **Tracing paper**
- **Black marker**
- **Black craft foam or black
  construction paper**
- **Black raffia, 10 inches
  (25 cm) long**
- **Nontoxic glue**
- **Scissors**
- **Craft knife**

1 Trace the outline of the spiderweb on page 17. Transfer it to the white drawing paper. Cut out the web shape and draw the inside lines of the web with the black marker.

On the black foam, trace the outline of the spiderweb pattern on page 17 and cut it out. Glue the foam spiderweb to the paper spiderweb.

2 Draw freehand or copy the small spider on page 17 onto the craft foam. Cut the spider out with the craft knife or scissors.

3 Glue the spider to one end of the raffia strand. Now glue the other end of the strand to the back of the spiderweb invitation.

Pumpkin invitation

- **Black miniflute corrugated cardboard, 10 × 7 inches (25 cm × 18 cm)**
- **Orange miniflute corrugated cardboard, 14 × 7 inches (35 cm × 18 cm)**
- **Orange poster board, 7 × 7 inches (18 cm × 18 cm)**
- **White glue**
- **Tracing paper**
- **Ruler**
- **Pencil**
- **Scissors**

1 Cut a square 7 × 7 inches (18 cm × 18 cm) in the black miniflute cardboard. Create two equal triangles by drawing and then cutting a diagonal line through the square. Starting from the base of one of the triangles, draw parallel lines 1 inch apart. Cut along the lines to create black strips. Follow the same steps using the orange miniflute corrugated cardboard.

2 Place the other black triangle on the plain orange poster board. Place the black and orange strips on the orange poster board as well, alternating colors to cover the entire surface. Glue the triangle and the strips to the orange poster board. Place a few heavy books over the card so that it dries flat.

3 Trace the outline of the pumpkin on the right. Transfer the pumpkin to what's left of the orange miniflute cardboard. Draw and cut out the pumpkin's eyes, nose, and mouth on the black miniflute cardboard. Glue the features to the pumpkin, and glue the pumpkin to the center of the card. You will need large envelopes to mail these cards.

Witch's hat invitation

- **Purple miniflute corrugated cardboard**
- **Black raffia fringe, 5 × 1 inches (12 cm × 2.5 cm)**
- **Tracing paper**
- **Gray construction paper**
- **Orange paper**
- **Black marker**
- **Photocopies of the drawings below**
- **Scissors**

Cut out a triangle, 6 inches high and 4½ inches at the base (16 cm × 12 cm), in the purple miniflute cardboard. Cut waves into the base of the triangle.

Glue the raffia fringe to the back of the base of the triangle.

Trace the bat below, transfer it to the gray paper, and cut it out. Draw eyes with the marker. Glue the bat to the top of the witch's hat.

Decorate the front of the hat with the photocopies of the bones and skeletons. Cut out and glue an orange triangle to the back of the witch's hat, and use it to write out your invitations.

Pop-up invitation

- **Orange card stock, 12 × 4 inches (30 cm × 10 cm)**
- **Black marker**
- **Black card stock, 8 × 8 inches (20 cm × 20 cm)**
- **Tracing paper**
- **Paper glue**
- **Scissors**

1 Fold the orange card stock in two lengthwise. Press down along the fold, then unfold the card and write "Halloween" on one of the inside flaps. Cut out two strips of black card stock, 1 inch × 8 inches (2 cm × 20 cm). Make accordion pleats with each strip. Leave about 1 inch (2 cm) between each pleat.

2 Glue the accordion strips to the right side of the card. On the black poster board, trace, then transfer the witch profile you prefer and the bat pictured on this page. Cut these out very carefully. Glue each figure to the end of a pleated strip.

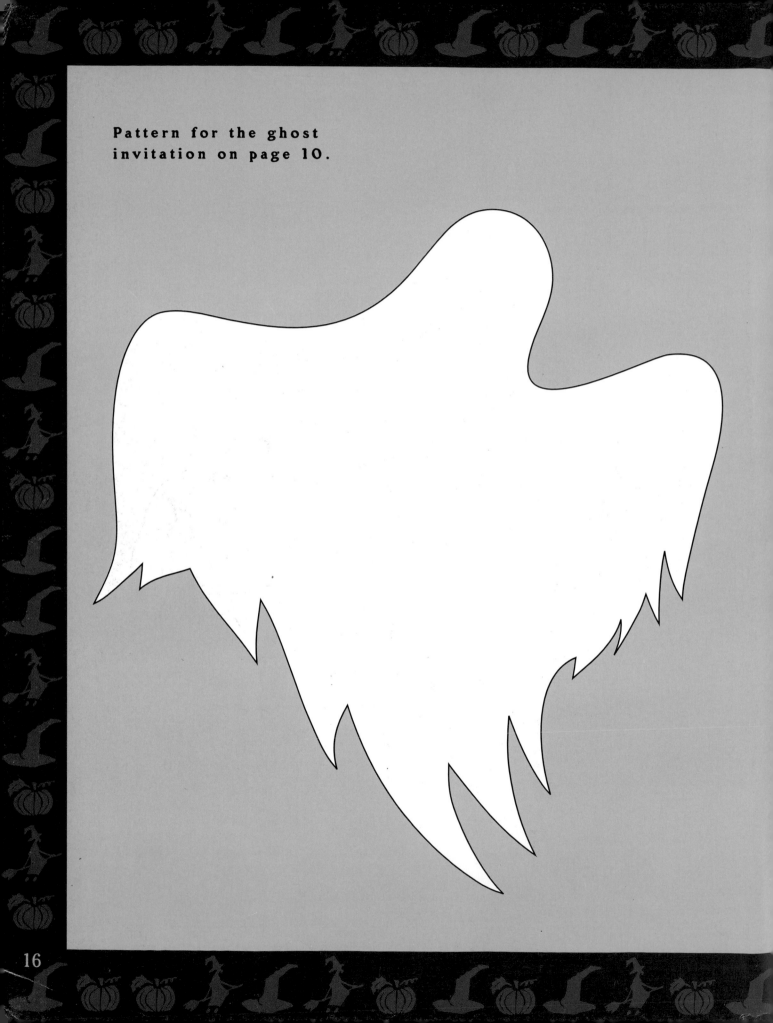

Pattern for the ghost
invitation on page 10.

Pattern for the spiderweb invitation
on page 11.

DEVILISH
WREATHS

A wreath fit for a witch

Tonight, nothing is impossible! Step up close to this witch's wreath if you dare. You just might find yourself totally bewitched!

- **Polystyrene foam wreath, 10 inches (25 cm) in diameter**
- **Black crepe paper strip, 2 × 60 inches (5 cm × 1.50 m)**
- **White mesh fabric or white abaca, 60 × 8 inches (1.50 m × 20 cm) (Abaca is available in millinery supply stores.)**
- **Tracing paper**
- **Orange card stock or poster board**
- **Black marker**
- **Black cord, 2 inches (5 cm)**
- **Craft bond glue**
- **Two sheets of Shrink Art Plastic**
- **White pencil**
- **Craft knife or plastic foam cutter**
- **Stapler**
- **Edging scissors or pinking shears**
- **Regular scissors**

1 Cut the polystyrene foam wreath in half so that you have two complete wreaths. Use a craft knife or other tool to complete this task.

Wrap the black crepe paper around one of the wreaths. Glue the paper at various points around the wreath to hold it in place.

Wrap the white abaca loosely around the wreath. Staple it to the underside of the wreath.

2 Trace and transfer the letters for "Halloween" reproduced on pages 22 and 23 to the orange card stock. Cut the letters out with the edging scissors and glue them to the wreath. Space the letters out evenly.

3 Trace and transfer the drawing of the pumpkin to the orange card stock.

Draw the pumpkin ribs with a black marker. Glue a little piece of black cord to the top of the pumpkin to make the stem. Glue the pumpkin to the wreath.

4 Place a sheet of Shrink Art Plastic directly on this page, keeping the rough surface toward you. Trace the cat first, then the spider on page 18 and the ghost on page 23. These figures will shrink after the Shrink Art Plastic has been cooked.

Color in the figures with the black marker and cut them out. Bake at 200–250°F (95–120°C) for about three minutes. Work quickly after you take the figures out of the oven, because they will harden almost immediately.

Glue the figures to the wreath with craft bond glue or a glue gun.

5 Trace the witch on page 23 with a black pencil. Transfer it to the black paper. Cut it out carefully and glue it to the top of the wreath.

A yummy wreath

This wreath has got to be magic. Are those candies real? Or part of the spell?

- **Rattan wreath, 10 inches (25 cm) in diameter**
- **Orange spray paint**
- **Quick-drying spray glue**
- **Black satin ribbon, 8 feet × 1 inch (2.40 m × 2 cm)**
- **Orange satin ribbon, 8 feet × 1 inch (2.40 × 2cm)**
- **8 small plastic bags (sandwich variety)**
- **3 tubes of little orange beads**
- **24 long black beads**
- **Orange cord, 12 inches (30 cm)**
- **Orange tulle, 40 × 1 inch (1 m × 2 cm)**

- **Black gift wrapping ribbon**
- **Black plastic lacing (Rexlace), 8 inches (20 cm)**
- **6 orange balloons, 6 black balloons**
- **6 small orange paper circles**
- **6 small plastic pumpkins**
- **3 pumpkin-shaped bells**
- **3 small black circles**
- **Skein of black raffia**
- **6 small transparent beads**
- **Narrow black satin ribbon, ¼ inch × 6½ feet (8 mm × 2 m)**

THE CANDIES
- **Assorted candies in colored wrappers**
- **Hard candies**
- **Licorice roll**
- **Gummy crocodiles**
- **Gummy bears**
- **3 licorice sticks**
- **6 round lollipops**

1 Lay the wreath on a sheet of newspaper. Paint it carefully with orange spray paint. Let it dry. Once the wreath is dry, turn it over and spray paint the other side. Let that side dry.

Cut the black satin ribbon into four pieces 2 feet (60 cm) long. Tie the ribbons into a bow around the wreath. Space the bows evenly.

2 Cut the orange ribbon into four pieces 2 feet (60 cm) long. Tie each piece of ribbon into a bow around the wreath, alternating black and orange bows.

Fill three small plastic bags with orange beads. Add eight black beads to each bag. Close the bags with a piece of orange cord about 4 inches (10 cm) long.

3 Fill the remaining five plastic bags with orange, green, or black candies. Close the plastic bags with a 1½-inch (4-cm) piece of plastic lacing or 8 inches (20 cm) of orange tulle.

Arrange the bags around the wreath and glue them to the wreath with the spray glue. If the bags are too heavy, use a piece of black gift wrapping ribbon to fasten them securely.

4 Tie one black balloon and an orange balloon together with a piece of black gift-wrapping ribbon.

Tape or glue the balloons to the wreath.

Glue the orange paper circles to the bows or to the plastic bags.

Fasten the pumpkins and the pumpkin bells to the wreath with black ribbon.

5 Make three little spiders by gluing a black paper circle on top of a dozen strands of raffia. Use two transparent beads for each spider's eyes. Place the spiders where they can easily be seen.

6 Now glue the hard candies, licorice rolls, gummy bears, gummy crocodiles, and all the remaining candies in the free spaces on the wreath. Make a pretty bow around the licorice sticks and fasten these to the wreath.

Stick lollipops between the strands of rattan.

7 To hang your wreath, tie a piece of black ribbon around a strand or two of rattan.

Tie the other end of the ribbon with a sturdy knot and hang your wreath from it.

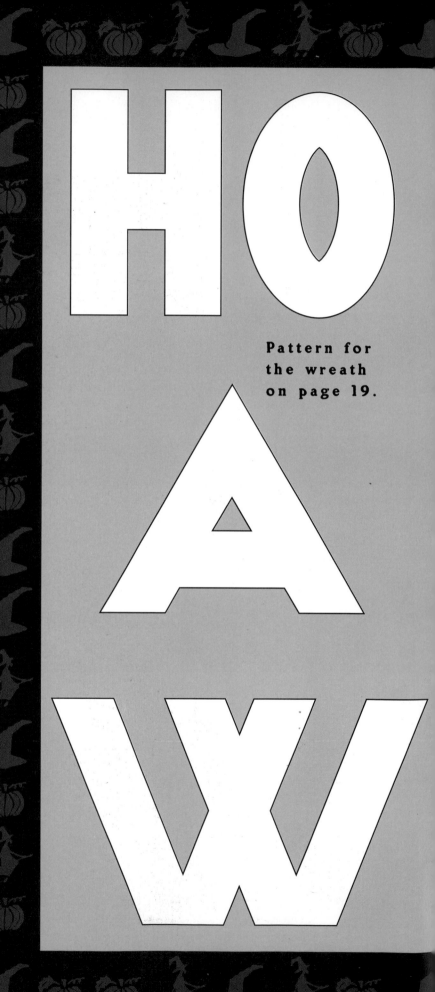

Pattern for the wreath on page 19.

Kooky kitchen stool

On Halloween night, witches get together and decide to turn innocent footstools into strange pieces of furniture. Try resting your back on this kooky stool!

- **Kitchen stool**
- **Straw broom**
- **Sandpaper**
- **Black satin paint**
- **Black spray paint**
- **Two nails, 1½ inches (4 cm)**
- **Polystyrene foam ball, 5 inches (12 cm) in diameter**
- **Black marker**
- **Paintbrush**
- **Hammer**
- **Craft knife**
- **Glue gun**

1 You may want to lightly sand the stool to make sure the paint will adhere to it. Paint the stool with the black satin paint. Let it dry.

Lay the broom flat on a piece of newspaper. Spray it with black spray paint.

When the paint is completely dry, turn the broom around and spray the other side.

2 Turn the broom upside down and hammer the broom handle to the stool with two nails. Make sure the nails go through the center of the handle to avoid splitting the wood.

3 Cut the polystyrene foam ball in two. Use one half to make a pumpkin. Carve pumpkin ribs into the ball with the craft knife.

Paint the ball orange: Let it dry, then draw two eyes, a nose, and a mouth on the ball with the black marker.

Use the glue gun to glue the pumpkin head to the broom.

Spiderwebs galore

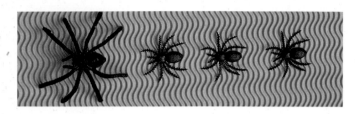

Weaving a spider's web is child's play. These spiders will be right at home in this web and look spookily real.

- **Four wooden craft picks**
- **Ball of thin string**
- **Quick-drying white glue**
- **Black acrylic paint**
- **Fine-point paintbrush**
- **Craft knife**

1 Use the craft knife to sharpen the ends of the craft picks. Make a cross with two picks and place a dab of glue where the picks intersect. Place the two remaining picks diagonally across the cross, one pick over and the other under the cross. Carefully tie the intersection of the craft picks with string and pull the knot tight.

2 Starting from the center of the cross, weave the spider's web in a spiral. Each time you get to one of the picks, wrap the string around it before going on to the next pick.

When you reach the outer edge of the web, wrap the string twice around the last pick and tie a knot.

3 Paint one side of the spider's web with acrylic paint, using a fine-point brush. Let it dry; then paint the other side the same way.

Spooky spiders

These spiders look so real, they're spooky. Make a whole bunch of them. They're easy to make and they don't cost much.

- Black felt square, 4 × 4 inches (10 cm × 10 cm)
- Wad of cotton
- Black thread, needle
- Two small round beads
- Black leather lacing or plastic lacing, 12 inches (32 cm)
- Scissors

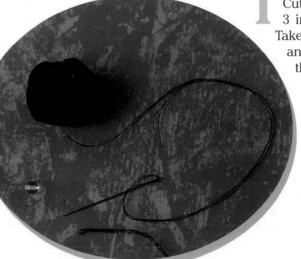

1 Cut a black felt circle about 3 inches (8 cm) in diameter. Take a small piece of cotton and place it in the middle of the felt circle. Pat the cotton into a ball.

Fold the felt over the ball to form the body of the spider. Close the seam with a few stitches.

2 To make the spider's legs, cut the black leather or plastic lacing into four equal pieces about 3 inches (8 cm) long. Place them evenly on the spider and stitch them to the body with the needle and black thread.

3 To make the eyes, stitch two small beads about ½ inch (1 cm) apart to the front of the body.

Frighteningly fat spiders

Are these hairy creatures about to crash your party? Or did you send them an invitation?

For one fat spider:
- **Steel wool pad**
- **Scrap paper**
- **Black spray paint**
- **Two transparent beads**
- **Quick-drying spray glue**
- **Two black pipe cleaners**
- **Scissors**

Use the scissors to cut the steel wool pad in two. Place one of the halves on a sheet of scrap paper and spray it with black paint. Turn the pad over and paint the other side. Make sure the pad is completely covered. Let it dry.

Put a drop of glue on the transparent beads and place them where you want the spider's eyes to be. Cut each pipe cleaner into three equal pieces. Curve each piece into an S-shape and extend one end to form the base of the spider's legs. Slip each leg into the black steel wool pad to create a spider with hairy legs.

Don't be fooled by these grinning balloons. They will cast creepy shadows on your walls.

For all the balloons:

- **Scissors**
- **Craft knife**
- **Black marker**
- **Hot-glue gun or aerosol craft bond glue**
- **Before you start this project, apply a little glue to one of the balloons. Some glues may cause the balloon to melt.**

Witch balloon

1 Blow up the balloon. Cut out both sides of the witch's pointed nose in the black foam. Make the pieces about 4 inches (10 cm) long.

Glue both halves of the nose together along the bridge and the tip. Fasten the nose to the middle of the balloon with a dab of glue.

Cut out two almond-shaped eyes with spiky eyelashes in the black foam. Glue them above the nose.

- **Green balloon**
- **Black craft foam, pink craft foam**
- **Skein of black raffia**
- **Two plastic spiders**

2 Cut out eyebrows, about 3 inches (8 cm) long, and a mouth in the pink foam. Glue these parts to the balloon face.

Now take the strands of raffia and glue them to the top of the witch's head. Make each strand about 40 inches (1 m) long.

Draw wrinkles on the witch's forehead and around her eyes. Make her even more repulsive! Glue the two plastic spiders to her face.

Cat balloon

1 Cut out cat ears in the black foam. Make the ears about 5 inches (12 cm) long. Cut two small black foam circles, each ½ inch (1 cm) in diameter.

Create a fabulous mustache by gluing several pieces of black straw to each circle. Allow the mustache to dry.

- **One black balloon**
- **White craft foam, black craft foam**
- **Pieces of straw from a straw broom**

2 Use the white foam to make the eyes and the nose. First, cut out two almond-shaped ovals 2½ inches (7 cm) long and draw pupils in the ovals with the black marker. Cut an equilateral triangle for the nose.

Blow up the balloon. Glue all the parts of the cat's face to the balloon with the glue gun.

You can hang the balloon easily using double-sided tape. Or make a loop with a piece of single-sided tape and stick it on your balloon.

Pumpkin balloon

- **Orange balloon**
- **Green fabric mesh or green abaca, 24 inches (50 cm) long**

Blow up the balloon and draw a grinning mouth, a nose, and two eyes with the black marker. You may use the pumpkin balloon pictured on the opposite page as a guide.

Roll the green abaca into a tight spiral. Create a funny-looking stem by gluing the spiral to the top of the pumpkin with the glue gun.

Spiderweb balloon

- **White balloon**
- **Small plastic spider**

Blow up the balloon and tie it tightly. Create a spider's web by drawing black lines in a star pattern, radiating from the center of the balloon.

Finish the web by drawing concentric circles around the black lines, starting from the center of the balloon. Try to copy the jagged lines shown on the photo.

Glue a creepy plastic spider to the middle of the web with the glue gun.

Jolly pumpkin candy bag

This smiley-faced pumpkin bag can't wait to be filled up with candies.

- **Orange felt square, 16 × 16 inches (40 cm × 40 cm)**
- **Black felt strip, 4 × 8 inches (10 cm × 20 cm)**
- **Green felt square, 2½ × 2½ inches (6 cm × 6 cm)**
- **Tracing paper**
- **Orange thread, black thread**
- **White fabric glue**
- **Black satin ribbon, 72 inches (1.80 m)**
- **Orange satin ribbon, 72 inches (1.80 m)**
- **Black braided cord, 40 inches (1 m)**
- **Pins**
- **Chalk**
- **Scissors**
- **Sewing machine**
- **Needle**

1 Fold the orange felt square in half. Hold the fabric together with pins.
Trace the pumpkin pattern on pages 34–35.
Cut out the pattern and pin it to the orange felt. Cut the pattern into the felt. You will have two pumpkins.

2 Trace the mouth, the eyes, and the nose that you like best from the shapes on pages 34–35. Place the features on the black felt and cut them out.

Fold the green felt in two. Trace the pumpkin stem on page 34 and cut it into the green felt. You now have two equal green pieces. Pin the pieces together. Do not pin the lower end of the stem. Attach this part of the stem to one of the pumpkins.

3 Stitch around the stem about ¼ inch (2 mm) from the edge.

Fasten both ends of the black cord about 5 inches (12 cm) apart to one of the pumpkins.

4 Cut the black and orange ribbons into three equal pieces about 24 inches (60 cm) each.

Pin the ribbons to the underside of the base of the pumpkin alternating orange and black ribbons.

5 Sew the two pumpkin heads together, using a stitch about ¼ inch (3 mm) from the edge. Leave an opening of about 5 inches (12 cm) from one end of the black cord to the other.

6 Finally, secure the eyes, the nose, and the mouth to the pumpkin head with the fabric glue.

Your bag is ready is be filled with the candies you like best for Halloween!

Pattern for the pumpkin candy bag pages 32–33.

Pattern for the mouth pictured on page 33.

Pattern for the pumpkin stem pictured on page 33.

Pattern for a mean-looking mouth.

Pattern for one of the eyes pictured on page 33.

Pattern for the nose pictured on page 33.

Pattern for a mean-looking eye.

String these garlands all over your house. They're so easy to make, you can hang them indoors and outdoors.

Pumpkin garland

- **Orange crepe paper**
- **Tape**
- **Photocopy of the pumpkin pictured below, enlarged 150%**
- **Two paper clips**
- **Pencil**
- **Scissors**

1 Cut strips of orange crepe paper 6 inches (15 cm) wide. Fasten the strips together with tape. The more strips you have, the longer your garland will be.

You now have one long strip. Fold the strip every 8 inches (20 cm) to make accordion pleats. Hold the strip folded with paper clips.

Cut out the pumpkin photocopy. Position the picture in the center of the strip. Outline the pumpkin in pencil.

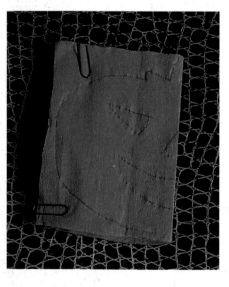

2 Fold the strip back so that each side shows one half of the pumpkin. This will make it easier to cut out the eyes, nose, and mouth. Hold the strip with the paper clips. Be careful not to cut too close to the edges. The pumpkins must be attached to each other when you unfold the garland.

Ghost garland

- **White crepe paper**
- **Tape**
- **Photocopy of the ghost below enlarged 150%**
- **Black marker**
- **Two paper clips**
- **Pencil**
- **Scissors**

Cut crepe paper strips 7 inches (18 cm) wide and fasten them together with tape. You will now have one long strip. Fold this strip every 7 inches (18 cm) to make accordion pleats. Hold the strip folded with paper clips.

Cut out the photocopy of the ghost and draw the outline on the crepe paper. Cut the ghost shape, but be careful not to cut the ends of his arms. The ghosts have to hold hands when you unfold the garland.

As a finishing touch after you have unfolded the garland, draw eyes and a mouth on each ghost, using the black marker.

Skull and crossbones cutouts

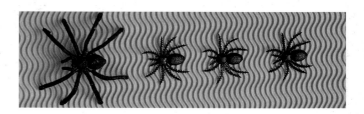

Inspired by Chinese cutouts, these skulls and crossbones are eager to be part of your celebration! Pirates ahoy!

- **Black tissue paper**
- **Tape**
- **Photocopy of the pattern on the opposite page, enlarged 110%**
- **Two paper clips**
- **White pencil**
- **Scissors**
- **Craft knife**

1 Cut the tissue paper into strips 8½ inches (22 cm) wide. Fasten the strips together with tape.
Fold the strip every 6¼ inches (16 cm) into accordion pleats. Hold the strip folded with paper clips.

2 Cut out the skull and crossbones pattern. Use the craft knife to carefully cut the white spaces out. Position the pattern on the folded strip; hold it in place with paper clips. Draw the pattern on the strip.
Cut the top and the bottom parts of the pattern with scissors. Use the craft knife to cut out the other areas. Remove the paper clips and carefully unfold the garland.

FESTIVE
LANTERNS

Halloween luminarias

There's nothing like candlelight to set a shivery scene. These lanterns will cast the scariest shadows on your walls.

- **Tart molds, 4 inches (10 cm) in diameter**
- **Wire mesh, 14 × 6 inches (35 cm × 16 cm)**
- **Orange spray paint, black spray paint**
- **Wire, 10 inches (25 cm)**
- **Bronze foil, 6 × 3 inches (15 cm × 8 cm)**
- **Tracing paper**
- **Pliers**
- **Black pencil**
- **Scissors**

1 Wrap the wire mesh around the tart mold. To close, fold one end of the wire mesh into the other with the pliers. Still using the pliers, fold ¾ inch (2 cm) of the wire mesh under the mold to hold it in place.

Make a handle by attaching the wire to both sides of the cylinder. Use the pliers to fold the ends of the wire around the mesh.

2 Place the lantern on a sheet of newspaper and paint it with black spray paint. Allow the paint to dry, then paint the other side of the lantern the same way.

3 Trace the pumpkin pattern pictured on page 42 and transfer it to the bronze foil.

FESTIVE **LANTERNS**

40

4 Use the scissors to cut out the bronze pumpkin.

5 Spray-paint one side of the pumpkin with orange paint. You may need to use two coats. Allow the first side to dry; then paint the other side.

Fasten the pumpkin to the lantern by folding the three tabs into the wire mesh.

6 You can choose to place votive candles or standard candles in the lantern. A little melted wax in the tart mold will hold the candles in place.

Be careful. Make sure you use a potholder when handling these lanterns. The handle and the wire mesh can become hot, especially if the candles have been burning for a long time.

Magic lantern

Another spellbinding idea: turn an ordinary plastic bottle into a devilish lantern!

- **Plastic bottle, preferably with a wide mouth**
- **Wire, 12 inches (30 cm)**
- **Black marker**
- **Flashlight, small, flat**
- **Craft knife**
- **Nail**
- **Pliers**

1 Use the craft knife to cut off the neck of the bottle.

Use the nail to make two holes opposite each other in the plastic. The holes should be about ½ inch (1 cm) from the top of the bottle.

Slip the wire through the holes to form the handle. To hold the handle in place, fold the ends of the wire with the pliers.

2 Cut an opening in the plastic, 1 × 3 inches (2 cm × 8 cm) from the bottom of the bottle. Slip the flashlight through the opening.

Use the black marker to draw eyes, a nose, and a mouth on the lantern. Create your own designs or use the photograph on this page as a model.

Be careful: do not put a candle into this type of lantern. The heat from the candle will melt the plastic and may cause a fire.

Pumpkins rule!

On Halloween night, when ghosts and spirits roam, every house must have a jack-o'-lantern in the window. These pumpkins rule the party!

- **Pumpkin**
- **Black marker**
- **Big kitchen knife**
- **Small kitchen knife**
- **Big kitchen spoon**
- **Fat candle on a base**

1 Draw a line to indicate where you will cut off the top of the pumpkin. The line may be jagged or follow the shape of the pumpkin. Make deep cuts in the pumpkin flesh with the big kitchen knife to remove the top.

Scoop out the pumpkin flesh with a big spoon. Remove all the seeds. Reserve the flesh, which you may want to keep for cooking.

2 Draw two eyes, a nose, and a big smiling mouth on the pumpkin with the black marker. Follow the model in the photograph.

Cut the pumpkin's features out with the small kitchen knife.

3 Place a big candle inside the pumpkin and it will glow with a jolly grin.

You may need a base for the candle to keep it steady. It also helps to make sure the bottom of the pumpkin is flat.

Pumpkin candlestick

A sneaky snake slithers across this pumpkin's head.

- **Orange self-hardening clay**
- **Gray self-hardening clay**
- **Wire, ¾ inch (2 cm)**
- **Scissors**
- **Craft knife**

1 Mold a hollow pumpkin shape out of the orange clay. Make sure the opening at the top of the pumpkin is fairly wide. Flatten the bottom of the pumpkin to create a base. Use the pointed tip of the scissors to carve pumpkin ribs into the clay. Carve the eyes, nose, and mouth out with the craft knife.

2 Roll the gray clay into a snake about 12 inches (30 cm) long. Use the blade of the craft knife to score scales along the body of the snake.

3 Make two eyes with the orange clay and a tongue with the ¾-inch (2-cm) wire. Drape the snake around the pumpkin and allow the candlestick to dry.

MENACING
M A S K S

Pumpkin mask

You don't need a complete costume to have a good time at your party. Just wear one of these masks. This pumpkin mask is the star of the show.

- **Orange miniflute corrugated cardboard, 10 × 12 inches (25 cm × 30 cm)**
- **Black braid, 48 inches (1.20 m)**
- **Black fringe, 8 inches (20 cm)**
- **Craft bond glue**
- **Black elastic hat ribbon, 10 inches (25 cm)**
- **Stapler**
- **Craft knife**
- **Pointed scissors**

1 Photocopy the pumpkin pattern on page 52. Cut out and transfer the pattern to the orange miniflute corrugated cardboard. Use the pointed scissors to cut the outline and the craft knife to carve the eyes, nose, and mouth.

2 Cut the black braid into six equal pieces, 8 inches (20 cm) long. Curl each piece and glue one end of each curl to the upper part of the mask. Make sure you glue the curls to the back of the mask.

Cut the fringe in half. Glue the fringes around the eyes to create enormous eyelashes.

3 Staple the elastic ribbon to both sides of the mask. Adjust it to fit your head.

Witch's hat mask

Frogs are jumping all over this witch's hat. Don't turn her away when she comes trick or treating at your door. She might cast a nasty spell on you!

- **Purple miniflute corrugated cardboard, 14 × 12½ inches (37 cm × 32 cm)**
- **Tracing paper**
- **Black miniflute corrugated cardboard, 11 × 10 inches (28 cm × 25 cm)**
- **Orange lightweight poster board, 4 × 6 inches (10 cm × 15 cm)**
- **Black marker**
- **Two oval-shaped orange candies**
- **Orange plastic funnel, 2½ inches (7 cm)**
- **Black raffia strands, 26 inches (65 cm)**
- **One round orange candy**
- **Black elastic hat ribbon, 10 inches (25 cm)**
- **Craft bond glue**
- **Scissors**

1 Draw a hat like the one pictured below on the back of the purple miniflute cardboard. Cut the shape out.

Trace and cut out the two frogs below on the orange cardboard. Draw their eyes with the marker. Glue the frogs to the hat.

Draw and cut out the witch's face on the back of the black miniflute cardboard. Glue the face under the hat with the craft glue. Draw and cut an oval-shaped mouth out of the orange cardboard. Add two rows of teeth with the marker. Glue the mouth to the mask. Glue the oval-shaped orange candies to form the eyes. Cut circles under the candies so you can see through the mask. Glue the funnel to the mask between the eyes to make the nose.

2 Glue about twenty strands of black raffia under the hat, on both sides of the face. To finish off your mask, paste the round orange candy on the witch's cheek, and glue tiny pieces of raffia to the candy. Now your witch has a horrible hairy wart!

To hold your mask in place, thread the elastic through two holes you have punched on both sides of the mask.

Skeleton mask

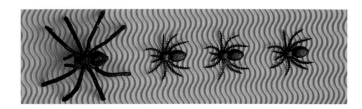

Skeletons will dance away when they come face-to-face (or bone-to-bone) with this mask. Is it too spooky even for them?

- **Light brown poster board, 8 × 10 inches (20 cm × 25 cm)**
- **Tracing paper**
- **Black marker, red marker**
- **Strip of black paper**
- **Strands of black raffia**
- **Small black paper circle**
- **Three small transparent beads**
- **White glue stick**
- **Elastic hat ribbon, 10 inches (25 cm)**
- **Scissors**
- **Craft knife**

1 Trace the pattern on page 53. Cut the pattern out, including the eyes and the nose, making sure the nose remains attached to the pattern. Now transfer the pattern to the light brown cardboard and cut the outline out.

2 Use the craft knife to carefully cut eyes and nose out of the cardboard. Make sure once again that the top of the nose remains attached to the skeleton's head.

3 Draw red and black circles around the eyes. Scribble lines all over the mask to look like sutures. You may use the photograph on this page as a model.

4 Create an earthworm by cutting zigzag lines along the strip of black paper. Glue on one transparent bead to simulate the worm's eye. Fasten the worm to the top of the skeleton mask with the glue stick.

All you need to do now is make the spider. Glue two transparent beads to the black paper circle. Glue a few raffia strands under the circle to look like spider legs. Fasten the spider to the skeleton mask with a dab of glue.

Staple the elastic ribbon to both sides of the mask.

Laughing pumpkin mask

There's nothing better than this laughing pumpkin mask to chase away the evil spirits on this special night. All you need is a paper plate and a little imagination!

- **Paper plate**
- **Orange paint**
- **Orange craft mesh or orange abaca, 40 × 4 inches (1 m × 10 cm)**
- **Craft bond glue or glue gun**
- **Orange burlap, 5 × 16 inches (12 cm × 40 cm)**
- **Orange thread**
- **Needle**
- **Green craft mesh or green abaca, 4 × 8 inches (10 cm × 20 cm)**
- **Felt spider (see pages 27 and 28)**
- **Elastic hat ribbon, 10 inches (25 cm)**
- **Black pencil**
- **Craft knife**
- **Stapler**

1 Paint the back of a paper plate orange. Allow it to dry.
  Draw the eyes, nose, and mouth of the pumpkin. Cut the features out with the aid of the craft knife.

2 Curl the orange craft mesh or orange abaca into waves. Dab glue at various points on the abaca to hold the waves. Glue the abaca to the unpainted side of the plate for a fancy headdress.

3 Fold the burlap in half along the width of the fabric. Create a wavy hairline for the pumpkin by threading the fabric and pulling lightly on the thread.
  Sew the burlap to the abaca headdress, using small stitches and the orange thread.
  Roll the green abaca into a long pumpkin stem. Glue this to the back of the plate.
  As a final touch, glue a felt spider to the orange burlap hair.
  Staple the elastic ribbon to each side of the mask. Adjust the ribbon if necessary.

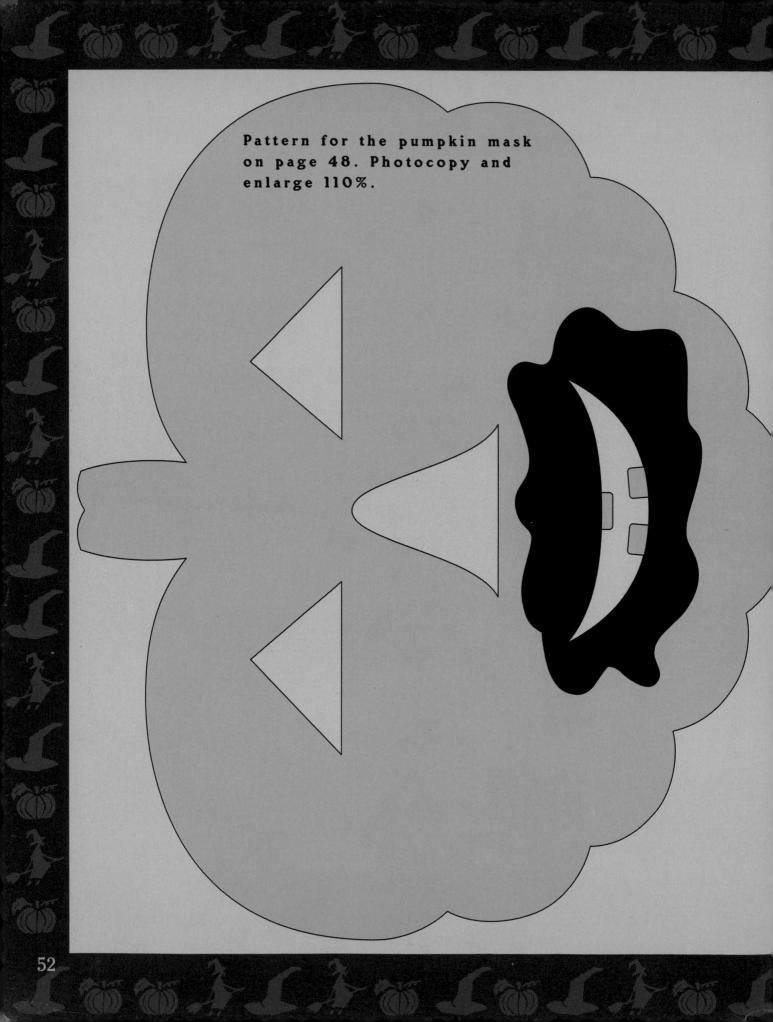

Pattern for the pumpkin mask
on page 48. Photocopy and
enlarge 110%.

Pattern for the skeleton head mask on page 50.

CREEPY
C O S T U M E S

The scariest witch gets it all on Halloween. This witch is sure to be given the most goodies by her friends and neighbors. Maybe it's the bewitching costume she's wearing.

The witch's dress

- **Black velvet, 86 × 55 inches (2.20 m × 1.40 m)**
- **Purple tulle, 80 × 36 inches (2 m × 90 cm)**
- **Black tulle, 63 × 36 inches (1.60 m × 90 cm)**
- **Black pipe cleaner, 51 inches (1.30 m)**
- **Black thread**
- **Pins**
- **Sewing machine**
- **Scissors**

1 Fold the velvet in two lengthwise to make the body of the dress. Now fold it again along the width. You should have a rectangle about 27 inches × 44 inches (70 cm × 1.10 cm). Pin the edges together to hold the fabric. Cut the neckline out according to the pattern shown here.

Cut out the sleeves and the sides of the dress. (The gray area in the picture represents the fabric you should cut away.)

Unfold the dress. Close the sleeves on each side with a stitch. Repeat for the sides of the dress.

Fold the dress again lengthwise. Make jagged sleeves and a jagged hem to the skirt by cutting into the fabric as shown on the pattern.

27 inches (70 cm)

44 inches (1.10 m)

2 To make the overskirt, cut a rectangular piece of purple tulle about 18 × 80 inches (45 cm × 2 m). Weave elastic sewing cord through the top of the skirt to create gathers. Close with a small snap.

Make the belt with a rectangular piece of purple tulle measuring about 12 inches × 27 inches (30 cm × 70 cm). For an accurate fit, measure your child's waist and add 2 inches (5 cm).

Fold the tulle in thirds. You will have a band about 4 inches (10 cm) wide. Press the creases with an iron. Stitch the pipe cleaner to the fabric with loose stitches about 1 inch (2 cm) from the top and the bottom of the belt. Staple the belt to the overskirt.

The hat

- **Black miniflute corrugated cardboard, 20 × 18 inches (50 cm × 45 cm)**
- **Three paper fasteners**
- **Purple tulle, 31 × 6½ inches (80 cm × 16 cm)**
- **Craft bond glue**
- **Purple braid, 12 inches long (30 cm)**
- **Pipe cleaner**
- **Piece of shell pasta**
- **Black gouache**
- **Black tulle, 29 × 80 inches (75 cm × 2 m)**

Roll the cardboard into a cone about 18 inches (45 cm) high. Close with the three paper fasteners. Fold the tulle into a strip 3 inches wide (8 cm). Weave an elastic sewing cord through the tulle to make a flounce. Glue this flounce to the underside of the hat.

Glue one end of the purple braid to the tip of the cone. To make the dangling spider, paint the shell pasta with black gouache. Allow it to dry. Cut the pipe cleaner into six equal pieces. Glue the pieces to the underside of the pasta. Glue the spider to the end of the braid.

3 The collar consists of one layer of purple tulle and one layer of black tulle. For the purple layer, cut a strip of tulle about 6 × 80 inches (15 cm × 2 m). Fold it lengthwise. Weave an elastic sewing cord through the collar about ¼ inch (5 mm) from the edge. When gathered, this layer should measure about 20 inches (50 cm).

To make the black collar, hem the black tulle about 2¼ inches (6 cm) from the edge. Thread elastic sewing cord through the hem. Stitch the collar closed along the width. Fold the hemmed part of this collar into the neckline of the dress. Slip the purple collar over it.

The broomstick

- **Broom handle**
- **Straw or twigs**
- **Raffia**
- **Black spray paint**

Tie the straw or the twigs to the broom handle with raffia. Wind the raffia around the handle several times and tie it with a sturdy knot.

Spray-paint the witch's broomstick black.

Witch makeup

- **Cosmetic sponge**
- **Face paint in white, green, gray, and black**
- **Fine-point paintbrush**
- **Green chewing gum**

1 Using the cosmetic sponge, apply white face paint to the forehead, bridge of the nose, cheeks, and chin. This will make the face and nose look longer and the chin pointier.

2 After rinsing the sponge, cover the white areas with a light coat of green paint, except for the chin and the nose. The witch will look quite sickly.

3 Shade the areas around the eyes, the sides of the chin, and sides of the nose with gray paint. Paint very black and hairy eyebrows with the paintbrush. Paint a few horizontal wrinkles across the forehead and dark circles under the eyes.

Outline the mouth in black paint, and turn the corners of the mouth down on both sides. Fill in the outline with more black.

4 A real witch has to have a wart on her nose! Stick a wad of green chewing gum over one nostril.

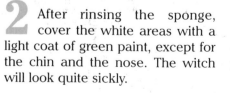

CREEPY COSTUMES

Tips for great makeup

You will need a cosmetic sponge. This is a special sponge that allows you to apply makeup evenly and in the amount you want. These sponges are best used damp, but be sure to wring out the excess moisture before you use them.

There are many kinds of face paints available. Choose one that is water-based and can be easily washed off after the party. Water-based paints are also easier to mix and produce more subtle shading.

Apply the paint directly to the skin with the sponge. Pat it on. This will help you avoid streaks.

In general, apply light colors first and darker colors over the lighter ones. Let the paint dry between applications, and be sure to wash the sponges and the brushes carefully when you change colors.

Consider having two different brushes, one flat-tipped and the other pointed. This will allow you to create a range of shapes and designs.

For detail work, hold the brush like a pencil and keep it at a right angle to the face.

To create a thicker line, apply gentle pressure to the brush as you move it along the face.

Face painting works best if you and the model sit facing each other. You will have a steadier hand, and the model will be less tempted to move.

Spider face

This design looks hard, but it's really easy. All in black and very attractive!

- **Black face paint**
- **Fine-point paintbrush**

1 This makeup requires a steady hand. Start the spider's web at a point between the eyebrows. Paint the lines going outward first and curve them slightly as shown in the photo. Continue painting until you have created a complete spider's web.

2 Finish the face by painting a beautiful long-legged spider on one cheek.

Remember to paint the mouth black too, using the fine paintbrush.

3 You need the right hairdo for the complete spidery look. Separate the hair into three sections. Make corkscrew curls with each section. Wrap each curl around itself. Fasten the curl to the head with hairpins. You may want to wrap a piece of pipe cleaner or black ribbon around each curl.

With one stroke of the magic wand, turn yourself into a cheerful, smiling pumpkin.

Pumpkin face

- **Cosmetic sponge**
- **Black, orange, and red face paint**
- **Fine-point paintbrush**
- **Thick-point paintbrush**

1 Apply orange face paint to the skin with a damp sponge. Do not paint around the eyes.

2 Use the fine-point brush to paint a black pointed arch over one eyebrow and a rounded arch over the other. Paint eyelashes under one eye and an inverted triangle under the other. Decorate the tip of the nose with a big black dot.

3 Define the eyes with black paint applied with a thick-point brush as shown in the photo above. Paint a big checkerboard mouth in black.

4 Use the thick-point brush to paint red ribs across the pumpkin's face.

Pumpkin costume

- **Orange beret**
- **Green craft mesh or green abaca, 4 × 8 inches (10 cm × 20 cm)**
- **Fabric glue**
- **Green felt, 24 × 24 inches (60 cm × 60 cm)**
- **Orange T-shirt**
- **Orange tulle, 82 × 60 inches (2.10 m × 150 cm)**
- **Black tights**

1 The orange beret will be the top of the pumpkin. Roll the green mesh or abaca tightly to form the pumpkin's stem. Glue the stem to the middle of the beret with the fabric glue.

2 To make the collar, fold the green felt diagonally once, then fold it diagonally again. You now have a triangle. Cut a circle 3½ inches (9 cm) from the top of the triangle. Cut off the two remaining angles so that the base of the triangle now has rounded corners. Create the sepals of the pumpkin by cutting into the green felt as shown in the photo.

Cut one side of the collar so it can be slipped around the neck.

Attach the sepal to the orange T-shirt with a couple of well-placed stitches.

3 Fold the orange tulle in two along the width of the material. Puff it out and tuck it into the top of the tights.

You may want to add two little bracelets made from the leftover green felt to your pumpkin costume.

This ghost is a classic. It's not Halloween without him. Here he is trailing his ball and chain and ready to haunt your party.

Ghost costume

- **White fabric, 126 × 51 inches (3.20 m × 130 cm)**
- **Black felt, 8 inches (20 cm)**
- **Fabric glue**
- **Extra-large T-shirt, previously worn**
- **Pins**
- **White thread**
- **Scissors**

1 There are two parts to this costume: white fabric worn over a T-shirt to which you will add a pair of big sleeves. Start with the white fabric. Cut a piece about 90 inches (2.30 m) long. Fold it in half, along the width of the fabric. Pin the sides together to hold the fabric.

Make uneven cuts about 12 inches deep (30 cm) into the fabric every 8 inches (20 cm) to create a ragged hemline.

2 Cut out two oval-shaped eyes 2 inches (5 cm) long in the black felt. Cut a mouth in the felt about 4 inches (10 cm) long.

Glue the eyes and mouth to the sheet at about the same height as your face. Now cut two small circles through the felt and the sheet so that you can see your way around.

3 Fold what's left of the white fabric in half lengthwise. Cut along the width of the fabric to make two sleeves. Fold each sleeve in two again. Hold the fabric together with pins. Then make deep cuts into the sleeves as shown in the picture.

Cut off the sleeves of the T-shirt at the seams. Roll the seams back and pin the big sleeves to the seams. Stitch the sleeves to the T-shirt at the seams.

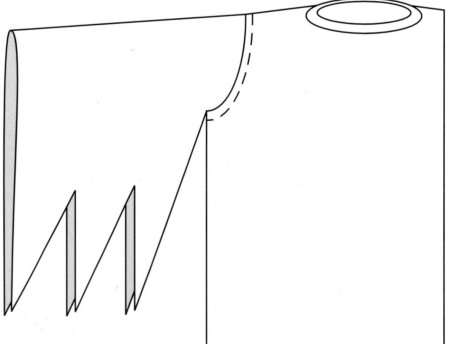

Ball and chain

- **Polystyrene foam ball, 6 inches (15 cm) in diameter**
- **Black spray paint**
- **Black crepe paper**
- **White glue**

Spray-paint the polystyrene foam ball black. Allow it to dry. To make the chain, cut twenty-five pieces of black crepe paper 6 × 1 inches (15 cm × 2 cm). Make a ring with the first piece of paper, close it with glue, then link the next ring around the first and glue that one closed. Continue until you have a long chain. Glue the end of the chain to the ball.

Allow the chain to dry for a couple of hours before you pick it up.

Cat face

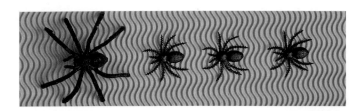

Watch out—this cat only looks sleepy. Actually, she's getting ready to pounce on any ghosts and goblins lurking about.

- **Cosmetic sponge**
- **Black, white, and orange face paint**
- **Fine-point paintbrush**
- **Thick-point paintbrush**

1 Apply white face paint around the mouth and above the eyes. Apply orange makeup over the rest of the face.

Dab a little white face paint on the cheekbones.

Define the eyes in black, making them as catlike as possible. Paint three long strokes over each eye to resemble cat eyebrows. Blacken the tip of the nose.

2 Paint a triangle between the nose and the mouth. Then paint three black ovals on both sides of the mouth. Paint cat whiskers coming out of these ovals.

Don't forget the hands! Apply orange paint to the top of the hand and paint pointy claws on it.

You can also create a cat hairdo. Make a ponytail on top of the head. Tie it with a black ribbon and allow a few strands of hair to fall loosely forward.

Vampire face

It's midnight and time for this vampire to climb out of his coffin. Watch out! He may be thirsty and you know what he likes to drink!

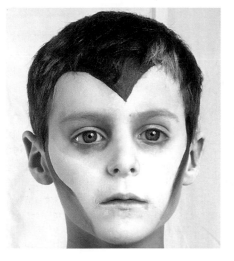

- **Cosmetic sponge**
- **Black, red, and white face paint**
- **Fine-point paintbrush**

1 Apply white paint with the cosmetic sponge, avoiding the area around the eyes. Apply the paint very evenly, especially on the cheeks.

Create hollow cheeks by painting black sideburns all the way down the upper jaw. Apply gray paint below the sideburns and along the cheeks.

Paint a pointy hairline on the forehead and fill it in with black paint.

To make this vampire even creepier, give him two eyebrows in different shapes. Then lightly paint dark lines under his eyes.

This makeup needs a light touch, so use a fine paintbrush throughout.

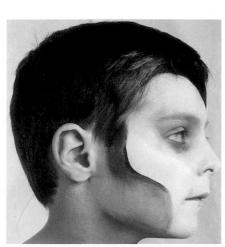

2 Starting from just above the nostrils, paint two dark wrinkles on each side of the nose.

Outline the mouth in black and fill it in with red. You may want to paint a trickle of red outlined in black on both sides of the mouth for a truly scary face.

Haunted castle

This is just the beginning of the story. You can invent the most fantastic goings-on behind the walls of this haunted castle.

- **Cosmetic sponge**
- **Light pink, light blue, dark blue, gray, brown, black, white, and red face paint**
- **Fine-point paintbrush**
- **Thick-point paintbrush**

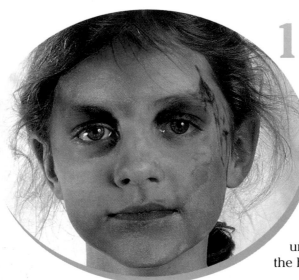

1 Start by applying light pink face paint with a dry sponge across the middle of the face. Sketch the outline of the castle on the face before applying light blue paint to the forehead and across the lower part of the face. Apply a thin layer of gray paint across the chin and lower cheeks and a layer of brown paint over that. Apply darker blue on the eyelids, under the eyes, and right below the hairline from ear to ear.

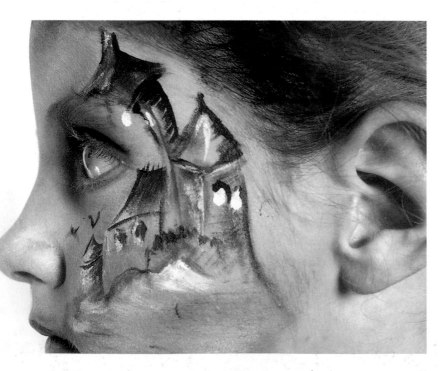

2 With black paint and a fine paintbrush, draw the castle on the cheek, using the photo on the left as a guide.

Apply touches of white paint to the windows of the castle and along the windswept dunes.

Apply touches of red to the windows in the main part of the castle. Surely something gruesome is happening inside.

Finish the makeup by painting the lips blue with the fine brush.

3 If your child has long hair, fluff it up, pull it back, and make a tight bun at the back of the head. Use your fingertips to add a little blue paint to a few strands in front. Use gel to hold the hairdo in place.

WEIRD

At the witch's table, even the plates are weird. You can share these pumpkin plates with your friends at your party.

Pumpkin plates

- **Clear glass plates**
- **Four photocopies per plate of the pumpkin pictured below**
- **Acrylic paint, light orange, dark orange, light green, dark green**
- **White craft glue**
- **Colorless nail polish**
- **Liquid non-toxic glaze**
- **Craft knife**
- **Paintbrush**
- **Rag**
- **Toothbrush**

1 Cut out the photocopies and glue four pumpkin pictures to the back of each plate with the white craft glue. Make sure the design shows through the plate. Carefully remove any extra glue and use the rag to smooth out air bubbles. You may need to make small cuts to each pumpkin so that they fit perfectly over the rim of the plate. Let dry twenty-four hours.

2 With a paintbrush, apply a fine coat of nail polish around the edges of the pumpkins so that the designs stay flat.

3 To create a plate with a green background, spread a thin coat of dark orange paint over the back of the plate with the toothbrush. Once the paint is dry, paint the center of the design, the pumpkin stems, and the area between the pumpkins in dark green.

4 Paint the rim of the plate in light green. Use brushstrokes that start at the rim and move outward, so that the paint appears to stream toward the edges. Let dry.

5 To make a plate with an orange background, spread a thin coat of dark orange on the back of the plate with the toothbrush. Paint the center of the design in pale orange and the rim in dark orange. Paint the pumpkin stems green.

6 Using the paintbrush, spread three coats of glaze over the painted side of the plates. This will ensure that the designs and the paint are permanently fixed to the plate.

Let the glaze dry for at least one hour between each application and twenty-four hours before you use them. The glaze may turn milky white when applied. This will disappear once it is dry.

Witch table decorations

- Tracing paper
- Bristol board
- Pencil
- Big markers, black, purple, and orange
- Polystyrene foam balls, 2 inches (5 cm) in diameter
- Orange gouache
- Scissors
- Craft knife
- White craft glue

1 Trace one of the witches shown on this page. You will find the same pattern in a larger size on page 23. Transfer the pattern as often as you like onto the bristol board.

Cut the witch shapes out with a craft knife. Pay special attention to the witch's broom since this feature of the design is harder to cut.

Color each witch on both sides with a marker.

2 Using the craft knife, cut the polystyrene balls in two. Paint each half orange.

Make a cut into the top of each ball with the craft knife.

Apply glue to both sides of the witch's feet and slip the feet into the cut. Angle the witch so that she is tilted slightly forward. Allow to dry.

Festive straws

Halloween straws are not for every day. These straws will add a spooky touch to all the drinks at your party.

- Orange, purple, green straws
- Craft foam in black, orange, green, white
- Tracing paper
- Beads
- Nontoxic glue
- Colored pencil
- Black marker
- Craft knife

1 Trace the pumpkin, witch, bat, or ghost patterns on pages 12–16 of this book. Transfer the patterns to the foam and cut them out with the craft knife.

You may add eyes by gluing beads or small circles cut out of craft foam.

2 There are two ways to attach these decorations: glue them to the straw with nontoxic glue or make two small cuts in the foam about ¼ inch (5 mm) apart and slip the straw through the cuts.

Table mats that look like ruined towers, and knife-holders made of bones. Are you still hungry?

Bat napkin ring

- **Black cardboard, 11 × 3½ inches (28 cm × 9 cm)**
- **Craft knife**
- **White pencil**

Trace the pattern on this page and transfer it to the black cardboard.

Use the craft knife to cut out the bat pattern. Close the napkin ring by fitting the notches into each other.

Spider napkin ring

- **Two black pipe cleaners**
- **Round pasta**
- **Black spray paint**
- **Two beads**
- **Glue gun or craft bond glue**
- **Scissors**

Cut a piece of pipe cleaner about 8 inches (20 cm) long. Make a ring by joining the ends of the pipe cleaner together.

Use the remaining pipe cleaners to make six spider legs about 1¾ inches (4 cm) long.

Paint the pasta black and allow it to dry. Glue the six legs under the pasta. Attach two beads to the head of the spider to make eyes. Finally, glue the spider to the napkin ring.

Serpent napkin ring

- **Orange pipe cleaner, black pipe cleaner**
- **Wire, 1¾ inches (4 cm)**
- **Two transparent beads**
- **Hot-glue gun**

Roll 1 inch (2 cm) of the black pipe cleaner into a ring to make the head of the snake. Twist together the black and orange pipe cleaners to form the body.

Carefully glue two beads to the head of the snake. Bend the wire in two and glue the round end of the wire to the snake's head. Your snake will have a forked tongue!

Wrap the snake around the napkin for an unusual napkin ring.

Halloween table mat

- **Felt rectangle, 18 × 12 inches (45 cm × 30 cm)**
- **Tracing paper**
- **Black craft foam, white craft foam**
- **Black felt**
- **Dressmaker's chalk**
- **Fabric glue**

Use the picture above as a guide to draw a tower in the orange felt.

Trace ghosts, bats, black cats, and witches from the pictures in this book. Cut the figures out of black felt and craft foam. Use the fabric glue to glue the figures to the castle towers, and you'll have a haunted castle to eat on.

Bones

- **White self-hardening clay**
- **Very fine sandpaper**

Roll out a piece of clay 2½ (7 cm) long. Mold a small piece of clay into two balls to make the ends of the bones. Press into the center of each ball to create the bumps at the ends of the bones and attach these pieces to the bone.

Allow the bone to dry. Smooth the surface with sandpaper.

Pumpkin centerpiece

Pumpkins are so festive for Halloween. Here's one that will last for a long time. It can be used to hold a bouquet of flowers, an arrangement of autumn leaves, or some of your trick or treat goodies.

- **Inflatable balloon**
- **Plaster gauze strips, 1¾ inches × 49 feet (4 cm × 15 m)**
- **Orange acrylic paint, black acrylic paint**
- **Black felt**
- **Varnish**
- **Scissors**
- **Two paintbrushes**

1 Blow up the balloon, tie the end tightly, and cut it as close to the knot as possible.

Place the balloon on its side. Cut the plaster gauze into strips about 10 inches (25 cm) long.

Soak them in water for a few seconds and apply them to the surface of the balloon, making sure the strips overlap.

Allow an area at the top of the balloon to remain uncovered.

2 Lightly flatten the bottom of the balloon to create a stable base for the pumpkin.

Apply three more layers of plaster strips. Allow the pumpkin to dry for a day. Use scissors to snip around the top of the plaster strips to create a more even opening.

3 Make thick plaster strips by placing three plaster strips one on top of the other to form the pumpkin's ribs. Place each strip ½ inch (1 cm) apart, until the pumpkin is covered. Allow to dry.

4 Apply a last layer of plaster gauze to the entire surface of the pumpkin. Let this layer dry thoroughly.

5 Burst the balloon and remove it from the pumpkin.

Paint the pumpkin with orange acrylic paint and let it dry.

Use the black marker to draw the eyes, nose, and mouth. Fill in the outline with black paint.

Protect your pumpkin by applying two layers of varnish to the entire pumpkin, including the base.

To create a flower arrangement, place some flower foam in a sturdy plastic bag, fill it with flowers, and place the arrangement in the pumpkin. Just be sure water does not seep out into the plaster.

Pumpkin tart

6 to 8 portions
- 1 deep-dish 9-inch pie crust
- 1 (15-ounce) can pumpkin puree
- ¾ cup sugar
- ½ teaspoon salt
- 1 teaspoon ground cinnamon
- ½ teaspoon ground ginger
- 2 eggs
- 1 cup whipping cream
- 1 (8-ounce) can almond paste
- Green food coloring

Preheat oven to 425°F (218°C). Place pie crust in oven and partially bake for 5 minutes. Remove and set aside.

In a bowl, beat together pumpkin puree and sugar. Stir in salt, cinnamon, and ginger. Add eggs and beat well. Stir in whipping cream.

Pour pumpkin mixture into crust. Place on cookie sheet. Bake for 15 minutes. Reduce temperature to 350°F (180°C) and bake another 40 to 50 minutes, or until filling is set.

Remove from oven and cool completely. Knead almond paste until soft. Add a few drops of green food coloring. Knead until paste turns green. Decorate tart with almond paste using the illustration at right.

Green spiders

12 portions
- 1 (8-ounce) can almond paste
- Green food coloring
- Licorice strings
- 24 cinnamon hot candies

Scoop out almond paste by the level tablespoon. Work in 2 to 3 drops green food coloring to tint the spiders. Shape paste into ovals.

Cut 6 (1-inch) pieces of licorice and fit into the almond paste to form legs. Press in 2 cinnamon candies to form eyes. Repeat with remaining ovals.

Chocolate skeleton

20 portions

- 3⅓ cups flour
- 2 cups light brown sugar
- ½ cup cocoa, plus extra for dusting
- 2 teaspoons baking soda
- ½ teaspoon salt
- 2 cups water
- ⅔ cup vegetable oil
- 2 teaspoons cider vinegar
- 2 teaspoons vanilla extract
- 1 (8-ounce) can almond paste

Preheat oven to 350°F (180°C).

In bowl of an electric mixer, combine flour, brown sugar, ½ cup cocoa, baking soda, and salt.

Add water, oil, vinegar, and vanilla. Beat for 2 minutes. Pour into greased and floured 9 × 13-inch pan. Bake in oven for 35 to 40 minutes or until toothpick inserted in cake comes out clean. Cool.

While cake cools, knead almond paste and roll into thin strips that you will use to make the skeleton.

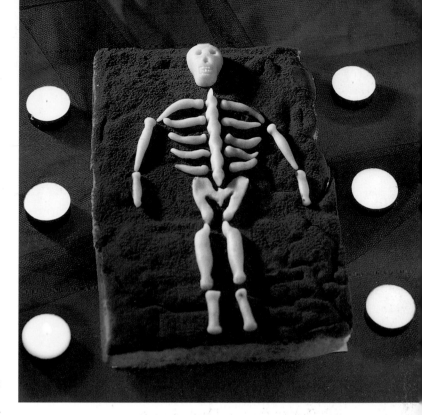

Sprinkle cake with cocoa and have fun placing the skeleton bones on top. Use the accompanying photograph as a guide to position each bone in the right place!

Spiders good enough to eat

12 portions

- 2 (3-ounce) bars bittersweet chocolate
- 2 tablespoons crème fraîche
- 2 tablespoons butter
- Chocolate sprinkles
- Licorice strings

In the top of a double boiler over simmering water, combine chocolate and crème fraîche. Stir with a wooden spoon until mixture melts. Remove from heat. Cut butter into small pieces and stir into chocolate until melted. Refrigerate for 3 hours or until chocolate is solid.

To form the spiders, take a tablespoonful of the mixture and pat it into a small ball with a spoon. Roll the ball in the chocolate sprinkles.

Cut the chocolate strings into 6 equal parts. Press 3 strings into each side of the chocolate-covered ball to

make the spider legs. Use the candies to make the spider's eyes. Your friends won't believe how delicious chocolate-covered spiders can be!

Here's a Halloween table full of weird and totally delicious things to eat. A skeleton presides over this banquet of edible spiders, snakes, and pumpkins.

You can create a lollipop bush for your children's table by placing 20 lollipops in Halloween colors in a plastic pumpkin head.

Pass a skewer or wooden craft pick through soft candies to create candy kebabs. Use a variety of colors to create an inviting array and place the picks in a pumpkin head. A flowerpot filled with flowers made from coconut balls looks magical on the treat-laden table.

That stuff dripping down the sides of the glasses? It's frosting (recipe page 78) dribbled along the rim when the glasses are warm. Strange candies in the form of dentures give the glasses an especially creepy look.

Do not hesitate to add spiders, snakes, and other plastic beasts to decorate the table and scare your guests.

The pitcher in the background contains a witch's brew specially made for this occasion. Mix 1 quart limeade and 1 quart green-colored soda. Use the back of a spoon to pour ½ cup of red grenadine syrup into the mixture. The grenadine will remain on the surface and produce a weird red coating over the drink. Makes 6 portions.

Spiderweb cake

6 portions

For the cake:

- **2 cups flour**
- **1¼ cups sugar**
- **1 tablespoon baking powder**
- **½ teaspoon salt**
- **5 tablespoons margarine, softened**
- **1 cup milk, divided**
- **1 teaspoon vanilla extract**
- **2 eggs**

For the frosting:

- **1 cup unsalted butter**
- **1½ teaspoons mint extract**
- **4 cups sifted confectioners' sugar**
- **4 to 6 tablespoons milk**
- **4 to 6 drops green food coloring**

For the decorations:

- **5 chocolate licorice strings**
- **Chocolate sprinkles**

Preheat oven to 350°F (180°C). Butter a 1-inch-deep, 9-inch round cake pan. Dust with flour and shake out the excess. Set aside.

In bowl of electric mixer, sift together the flour, sugar, baking powder, and salt. Add the margarine, ⅔ cup milk, and vanilla. Beat at medium speed for 2 minutes.

Add the remaining milk and the eggs. Beat for 2 minutes.

Pour batter into pan and bake for 45 minutes or until toothpick inserted near center comes out clean.

Remove cake from pan. Let cool 10 minutes, then turn out onto rack and cool completely.

Prepare frosting. In bowl of electric mixer, beat together butter, mint extract, and confectioners' sugar until creamy.

Now add a few drops of green food coloring until you have a color you like. When the cake has cooled, spread the butter frosting evenly over the top with a spatula.

Press chocolate sprinkles into the sides of the cake. Create a spiderweb with the chocolate licorice strings. Keep well chilled until ready to serve.

Haunted castle

- **2 (16-ounce) cans vanilla frosting**
- **Confectioners' sugar**
- **Green food coloring**
- **1 (7.5 oz) package Petits Beurre crackers**
- **1 (12-ounce) package long, oblong cookies**
- **4 rolled cookies (Pirouette)**
- **1 (12- to 16-ounce) package sugar wafers**
- **8 to 10 ice cream cones**
- **Assorted candies**

To make a stiff frosting, combine the canned frosting in bowl of electric mixer. Add enough sugar, by the half-cup, to make a frosting that stands up. Add 3 to 4 drops green food coloring to tint.

You will need a flat surface on which to build the castle, such as a piece of cardboard covered with aluminum foil.

Build the four walls with two layers of Petits Beurre crackers, following the photograph. Cement the cookies in place with the frosting. Building the walls will be easier if you have a milk carton or a rectangular shape in the center to hold the walls up until the frosting hardens.

Place the long, oblong cookies at the point where the layers of cookies meet. Hold these together with frosting.

To create the spiky gate, place a few upright rolled cookies and hold these together with frosting.

Now build the castle's roof, using two rows of sugar waters. Seal the sugar wafers together with frosting.

Create turrets by placing the cones upside down on the four corners of the castle. Hold these together with frosting.

A finishing touch: Add candies in Halloween colors to the structure. Personalize your castle with jelly beans, gummy snakes, even candies shaped like ghosts.

Monster kebabs!

Children will love these monster kebabs.

Choose candies soft enough for the wooden picks or skewers to go through. Use about 8 to 10 candies per skewer. Vary the colors and the types of candies, using your imagination and your child's preferences.

If possible, find a candy shaped like a spider, ghost, or pumpkin to top off the kebab.

Halloween canapés

20 portions
- 10 slices white bread
- 1 (8-ounce) jar tapenade (a paste made of anchovies, capers, and olives, available in gourmet groceries)
- 2 carrots

Remove the crust from the white bread. Use a 2-inch cookie cutter to cut the bread into 20 rounds.

Spread ½ tablespoon tapenade on each round of bread.

Slide the carrots into rounds and place a carrot round on each canapé. Top the canapé off with a dollop of tapenade.

To turn toothpicks into witches' broomsticks, wrap black raffia around the toothpicks, and fasten with a piece of plastic wire.

Red cabbage and orange sections salad

10 portions
- 6 cups sliced red cabbage
- 2 oranges
- 2 cups seedless black grapes
- ¼ cup each cider vinegar, canola oil, olive oil
- Salt and pepper to taste

Peel and section the oranges. Add to cabbage. Place cabbage in bowls.

Wash the grapes and stem. Add to cabbage.

Prepare a vinaigrette using salt, pepper, vinegar, canola oil, and olive oil. Dress the salad just before serving.

Pumpkin soup

6 portions
- **1 (15-ounce) can pumpkin puree**
- **½ teaspoon ground cinnamon**
- **¼ teaspoon ground ginger**
- **2 cups milk**
- **¾ teaspoon salt**
- **¼ teaspoon pepper**
- **3 tablespoons crème fraîche**
- **2 hard-boiled eggs**
- **1 ripe olive**

In a medium pot, combine pumpkin puree, cinnamon, ginger, milk, salt, and pepper. Simmer 10 minutes, or until soup is hot and spices are blended.

Stir in crème fraîche and cook over very low heat for 5 minutes or until crème fraîche blends in. Do not allow soup to boil.

Add a creepy detail: two eyes floating on the surface of the soup. Place the hard-boiled eggs gently on the soup so they float. Then add two tiny pieces of olive to each egg to form eyes.

This witch has prepared a bewitching buffet. Luckily, she is willing to share her magic formulas with you, and, with a wave of her wand, help you create a spectacular banquet like hers!

Lit only by the mysterious lights of a candelabra, this buffet for grown-ups must be the work of deliciously wicked spirits.

An enormous spiderweb appears to cover the table. It looks as if it's been there for centuries. Toothpicks have handles made of clay bones; lanterns wrapped in orange tissue paper spread a soft glow that harmonizes with the flickering candlelight.

Punch is served in a cauldron made from a round aquarium, painted orange and stenciled with streaks of black paint.

For a successful Halloween party, all you need is a few magical ideas and a sense of fun!

Black pasta and calamari salad

8 portions
- 1 (12-ounce) package squid ink fettuccine
- Salt
- 6 eggs
- 1 cup canned, diced beets
- 8 ounces frozen, thawed, and cooked squid rings
- ½ cup diced cheddar cheese
- ⅓ to ½ cup olive oil
- 3 to 4 tablespoons red wine vinegar
- ½ teaspoon pepper
- ½ teaspoon crushed, dried tarragon
- ¼ teaspoon crushed, dried thyme

Cook pasta in boiling water until just tender. Drain and set aside.

Place eggs in pot with water to cover. Bring to the boil. Reduce heat to low and simmer 5 minutes. Remove from heat and hold eggs under cold running water. Peel and place in a bowl with chopped beets, stirring to tint eggs red.

To serve, place pasta in a large bowl. Add eggs, beets, squid rings, and cheese.

In a cup, stir together oil, vinegar, 1 teaspoon salt, pepper, tarragon, and thyme. Stir well. Just before serving, pour dressing over pasta. Toss gently but well.

Pumpkin flan

6 portions
- 1 (15-ounce) can pumpkin puree
- ½ cup whipping cream
- 2 tablespoons flour
- 1 teaspoon salt
- ½ teaspoon paprika
- 3 eggs, beaten
- ½ cup grated Swiss cheese

Preheat oven to 325°F (165°C).

Combine pumpkin puree and cream in a small pot. Bring to a simmer. Place flour in a cup. Stir in ¼ cup pumpkin mixture, stirring until smooth. Add flour mixture back to pumpkin. Remove from heat. Stir in salt and paprika. Add eggs and mix until smooth.

Pour the mixture into an oven-proof 1½-quart dish. Top with grated cheese. Bake for 45 minutes to 1 hour. You may want to decorate the flan with plastic spiders but be careful not to eat them!

Orange cake

8 portions

- ½ cup butter
- 1 cup sugar
- 2 egg yolks
- 2 cups flour
- 2 teaspoons baking powder
- ½ teaspoon baking soda
- 1 tablespoon grated orange rind
- ¾ cup orange juice
- 1 (8-ounce) can almond paste
- Red, green, and yellow food coloring
- 1 (16-ounce) can white frosting
- Candies in various colors
- 2 licorice candies

Preheat oven to 350°F (180°C). Butter a 1-inch-deep, 9-inch round cake pan. Dust with flour and shake out the excess. Set aside.

In a mixing bowl, cream butter. Add sugar gradually and beat until creamy. Add egg yolks, one at a time, beating after each addition. In a bowl, stir together flour, baking powder, and baking soda. In a small bowl, stir together orange rind and juice.

Alternately add flour mixture and orange juice to butter, beginning and ending with flour.

Spoon batter into prepared pan. Bake for 35 minutes or until toothpick inserted near center comes out clean. Remove cake from pan. Let cool 10 minutes, then turn out onto rack and cool completely.

Place almond paste in a bowl and knead until soft. Color the paste with a few drops of yellow and red food coloring until it turns orange. Roll out paste with a rolling pin.

Cut a circle in the almond paste slightly bigger than the cake. Place this circle over the cake and fold the edges down.

Decorate the cake with almond paste tinted green. Cut out triangles for the eyes, nose, and stem of the pumpkin and create a mouth.

Use a pastry bag filled with white frosting to create the ribs of the pumpkin.

Prunes stuffed with almond paste

40 portions

- 1 (12-ounce) package pitted prunes
- 1 (8-ounce) can almond paste
- Orange food coloring
- Chocolate licorice strings

Spread prunes open.

Shape the almond paste into ovals, using 1 scant teaspoon for each. Place a piece of almond paste in each prune. Press the sides of the prunes together to close.

Decorate with a variety of creatures made of almond paste: add a few drops of orange food coloring and a few chocolate licorice strings to make a spider, or place a few red dots on the almond paste, or prop a smiling pumpkin on top of a prune.

Witch's cake

10 portions

For the cake:

- ½ cup butter
- 1 cup sugar
- 3 eggs, beaten
- ½ teaspoon almond extract
- 2 cups flour, sifted
- ¼ teaspoon salt
- 1 teaspoon baking powder
- 1 teaspoon baking soda
- 1 cup milk
- 1 teaspoon cider vinegar

For the frosting:

- 1 cup butter
- 2 teaspoons almond extract
- 4 cups confectioners' sugar
- 4 to 6 tablespoons milk
- Green and blue food coloring

For the decorations:

- Almond paste
- Colored sugar crystals: black, purple, orange
- Orange, black, green candies

Preheat oven to 350°F (180°C).

Butter a 1-inch-deep, 9-inch-round cake pan. Dust with flour and shake out the excess. Set aside.

In the bowl of an electric mixer, beat butter and sugar until light. Add eggs and beat until well mixed.

Stir in almond extract.

In a bowl, stir together flour, salt, baking powder, and baking soda. In a second bowl, stir together milk and vinegar to sour the milk.

Alternately add flour mixture and milk to the batter, beginning and

ending with flour. Pour batter into prepared pan. Bake for 30 minutes or until toothpick inserted near center comes out clean. Remove cake from pan. Let cool 10 minutes, then turn out onto rack and cool completely.

To make the frosting, combine butter, almond extract, and confectioners' sugar in bowl of electric mixer. Beat in enough milk to make a light frosting. Divide this mixture into two equal parts and spoon into separate bowls. Add a few drops of blue food coloring to one bowl, a few drops of green to the other.

Now cut the cake in the shape of a witch. Spread butter cream over the surface of the cake using green frosting for the face, blue for the body. Dust the witch's dress with black sugar, the hat and the hair with purple sugar. Roll some almond paste into white strands on both sides of the witch's head. The eyes and the mouth are made of candies. Sprinkle orange sugar around the witch's collar and along her arms. Decorate the hem of her dress and the edge of the cake with colored candies.